Lost and Found...
Three Parables

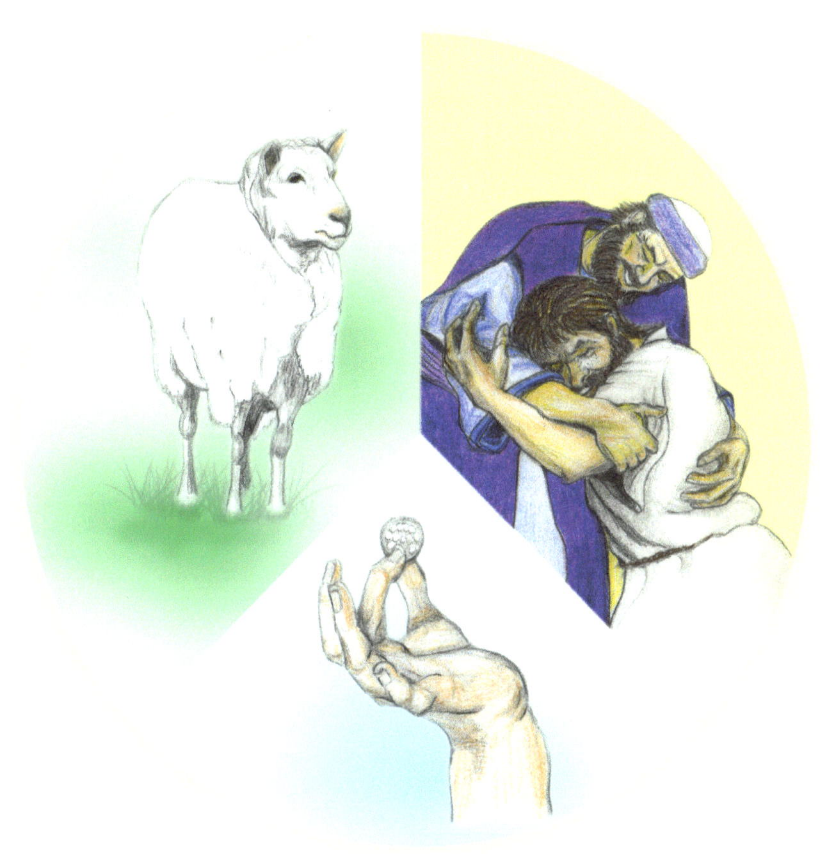

Cherie Wray
Illustrations by Cherie Wray

Copyright © 2019— Cherie Wray

All rights reserved

No part of this book may be reproduced or transmitted in any form or by
any means, graphic, electronic, or mechanical, including photocopying,
recording, taping, or by any information storage retrieval system, without
the permission, in writing, from the publisher.

ISBN: 978-0-692-0315-0
Printed in the United States of America

Dedication

To GOD, the Author and Creator of all things, be the Glory, for ALL the great things HE has done!

To my babes, near and far…
you are ALL welcome in HIS loving arms! Run home to JESUS, all who have wandered and are weary, and you will find peace and rest.

I am ever the wandering parable
of THE FATHER and HIS reckless child;
a willful, rebellious, prodigal son-
so demanding, so impatient, so beguiled!

But in compassion, arms open,
THE FATHER came running
to the object of heartache and prayer,

and in HIS delight, HE enfolded, forgave
this one saved from death's foul snare…

I am ever the lost treasure worth pursuing – a coin,
diligently sought for throughout …

all the lamps were lit, the rooms were swept,
the poor house was turned upside-down!

This dowry invaluable – a token so precious,
an inheritance beyond compare…

then it was heard, "I have found what was lost! Rejoice with me – come and share!"

I am ever the insensible sheep gone astray –
weary vagabond, wilderness bound;

indifferent to danger – so foolish, incapable
of finding my own way around.

This lost soul, THE GREAT SHEPHERD so lovingly
lays on HIS shoulders - HIS task so profound...

HE is not willing that any be lost,
earnestly seeking till all safe and sound!

In each of these parables -

the stray
sheep,

the lost
coin,

the prodigal son
homeward bound,

a company of neighbors and friends were all called -
the 'GOOD NEWS' to celebrate, they expound!

Each one in its
way represents
GOD everyday,

as persistently
seeking the
world 'round,..

All of heaven is jubilant
in the presence of THE LORD,
when all who are lost
have been found!

www.ingramcontent.com/pod-product-compliance
Lightning Source LLC
Chambersburg PA
CBHW042145030726
47599CB00002B/625